Globalize, Localize, Translate

Tips and Resources for Success

By

Thei Zervaki

ISBN: 0-7596-7567-8

This book is printed on acid free paper.

1stBooks - rev. 04/16/02

TRANSLATE, LOCALIZE, GLOBALIZE: TIPS AND RESOURCES FOR SUCCESS. A condensed guide of how to globalize web sites, documents and products for businesses, vendors and language professionals.

To my mother
to my family
and to my global friends.

TABLE OF CONTENTS

1. GLOBALIZATION - THE CONCEPT 1
   1.1. Is Globalization new? 1
   1.2. What is globalization? 1
   1.3. The World Wide Web: Globalization's friend 2
   1.4. Definitions: What is the WWW? 2
   1.5. English and the Internet 3
2. DEFINITIONS 6
   2.1. Globalization - the strategy 6
   2.2. What is internationalization? (abbreviation I18N) 7
   2.3. What is localization? (abbreviation L10N) 8
   2.4. Translation, your friend in the global market 9
3. TIPS FOR BUSINESSES
3.1. Do you need to localize? 11
   3.2. For web site localization 12
   3.3. Explore your options 12
      3.3.1. Localization needs organized in-house: 12
      3.3.2. Hiring a vendor 13
      3.3.3. Using freelancers 14
   3.4. How to choose a vendor 15
      3.4.1. What to check for in particular 15
      3.4.2. Some other issues you will have to address: 16
   3.5. Getting the budget 17
   3.6. The structure of pricing for translation 18
   3.7 Work on your English for global documentation 19
      3.7.1 Use plain English and be clear in style 19

3.7.2. Be culturally neutral 19

4. TIPS FOR TRANSLATION AGENCIES AND
LOCALIZATION VENDORS 21

    4.1. General advice for all vendors 21

    4.2. The translation test piece 22

    4.3. How to choose translators for your agency/company ... 23

    4.4. How to get clients 23

5. THE PROCESS OF PROJECT MANAGEMENT IN
TRANSLATION/LOCALIZATION INDUSTRIES 25

6. WEB CONTENT MANAGEMENT (in relation with the
marketing/localization or communications department) 28

7. COMPUTER AID TRANSLATION (CAT) 29

    7.1. Machine Translation 29

    7.2. Machine Assisted Human Translation (MAHT) 30

    7.3. Terminology managers 31

8. ONLINE TRANSLATION SERVICES 32

9. TIPS FOR LANGUAGE ISSUES: WHAT TO LOOK
FOR 33

10. TIPS FOR CROSS-CULTURAL AND LOCALIZATION
ISSUES: A FEW EXAMPLES 34

11. TIPS FOR TRANSLATORS/LINGUISTS 36

    11.1. Definitions 36

    11.2. Studies 37

    11.3. Going freelance 39

12. THE FUTURE OF LOCALIZATION 41

13. WHAT IS THE FUTURE FOR THE ENGLISH
LANGUAGE? 42

RESOURCES

1. LOCALIZATION COMPANIES 45
2. LOCALIZATION SPECIALISTS IN RARE
    LANGUAGES 50
3. WORKFLOW AND PROCESS MANAGEMENT 51
4. GLOBALIZATION STRATEGY CONSULTANTS AND
    SERVICE PROVIDERS FOR E-BUSINESS AND B2B 53
5. DOMAIN NAMES REGISTRATION 55
6. WEB CONTENT MANAGEMENT 56
7. CAT DEVELOPERS/ COMPANIES (MACHINE
    TRANSLATION, MEMORY TOOLS AND
    TERMINOLOGY MANAGERS) 57
8. SPEECH RECOGNITION/TEXT-TO-SPEECH
    SOFTWARE 62
9. ONLINE MACHINE TRANSLATION COMPANIES
    AND DEVELOPERS FOR WEB SITES, EMAIL AND
    BROWSERS. 64
10. ELECTRONIC DICTIONARIES AND
    MULTILINGUAL SOFTWARE DEVELOPERS
    (SPELLERS, DICTIONARIES, THESAURUS) 67
11. PORTALS USING ONLINE MACHINE
    TRANSLATION 68
12. LANGUAGE RESELLERS AND RESOURCES OF
    PRODUCTSTHE INTERNET CORPORATION FOR
    ASSIGNED NAMES AND NUMBERS 69
13. ON-LINE WORK PLACES FOR TRANSLATORS 70
14. MAJOR TRANSLATION COMPANIES/AGENCIES 71
15. LOCALIZATION ASSOCIATIONS AND
    ORGANIZATIONS 74
16. MACHINE TRANSLATION RESOURCES AND SITES 75

17. SITES FOR COMPUTATIONAL LINGUISTICS AND NLP 76

18. LANGUAGE RESOURCES 77

19. PUBLICATIONS/NEWSLETTERS 78

20. BOOKS 79

21. UNIVERSITIES AND COLLEGES OFFERING DEGREES OR COURSES IN LOCALIZATION 80

22. ETIQUETTE 81

23. INTERCULTURAL MANAGEMENT AND TRAINING 82

24. ONLINE CROSS-CULTURAL RESOURCES 83

25. USEFUL SITES FOR TRANSLATORS 84

26. USEFUL SITES FOR LINGUISTS 85

27. EUROPEAN UNION SPONSORED SITES RELATED TO LANGUAGE TECHNOLOGY 86

28. TRANSLATION SCHOOLS WORLDWIDE 87

29. TRANSLATORS ASSOCIATIONS 88

30. RESEARCH ENGINES IN DIFFERENT COUNTRIES 90

REFERENCES 93

ABOUT THE AUTHOR 95

GLOSSARY OF TERMS

ASP: Application service provider

CAT: Computer Aid Translation

GRL: Global, Regional, Local

I10N: Localization

I18N: Internationalization

LISA: The localization Industry Standards Association

MAHT: Machine Assisted Human Translation

MT: Machine translation

QA: Quality Assurance

TM: Translation Memory

Dynamic web sites: store content in a database so that it is completely separate from the code. They tend to be more difficult to create but it is easier to maintain and update. When changes are made in the source language (site), the technology developed detects and manages these changes into other languages (sites).

Static web sites: are structured so that content is stored with the HTML rather than in a database.

1.
GLOBALIZATION - THE CONCEPT

1.1. Is Globalization new?

No. The first and crucial event of globalization was the post World -War II removal of barriers to trade. Countries have become more open as a result and world trade growth has averaged two or three times the rate of growth of national output. In addition, international organization agreements for free trade and free movement of capital, goods, services and people have also had a major contribution to that. The end of the conflict between US and the Soviet Union, the collapse of most communist regimes made Capitalism the "only game around" in the Nineties.

Globalization, the most powerful symbol of today's capitalism, has come here to stay. As a consequence, large multinational companies account for one-third of world gross domestic product and two-thirds of world trade. The rich are getting richer and large corporations larger but many people have missed out on its benefits. 1.2 billion people, almost a quarter of the world's population, lives on less than a dollar a day. Another two billion are categorized as living "in poverty".

1.2. What is globalization?

The growing interdependence of the modern world through increased ease of movement of goods, services, capital, people, ideas and information. In other words, despite fears of Coca Colonization and fears for the McWorld (although the large corporation is clearly an aspect of it) and cultural homogenization, globalization means

1

that no country is an island in today's economy. Any action, however small, in one part of the world can have a direct effect on many other regions, countries and continents.

1.3. The World Wide Web: Globalization's friend

One means of globalization is the WWW and the Internet. The World Wide Web became popular in the mid nineties and since then millions of people in the world can access it with little money or for free. This information database is easily available with a modem connection, a browser and a PC, can spread information, facilitate communication and international sales of products. However, one element is crucial for its universal use: LANGUAGE.

1.4. Definitions: What is the WWW?

The World Wide Web is a global, seamless environment in which all information (text, images, audio, video) that is accessible from the Internet can be accessed in a consistent and simple way by using a standard set of naming and access conventions.

By using a web browser, you can access sites all over the world by just connecting from your desktop or laptop to thousands web servers. Then just click on a selection or enter a specific address.

The basis of the Web is the Internet. The web is built on the Internet.

Internet is the physical aspects - computers, networks, services. It allows to connect to thousands of other computers across the world. The Web, is the set of protocols and tools that let us share information with each other.

Why companies use the Web?

1. For external communication.
2. To share product information.
3. To learn about the market place.
4. To share in process work with business partners.
5. For internal sharing of information.

1.5. English and the Internet

Any one Internet user can easily have the impression that nearly all the world speaks or understands English. The language, is becoming a lingua franca, with all the benefits that this would bring for international communication. But it also threatens cultural diversity and independence.

English is everywhere: in film, pop music and television. The majority of international conferences and business, science and academic communications are all in English. In addition, the working language of the Asian trade group ASEAN and the official language of European Central Bank - even though the bank is based in Frankfurt. Is English typically the language of people who either come from richer nations, or is the second language used by a wealthy and influential professional elite. Hence its dominance.

As a consequence and coupled with the fact that the World Wide Web was first established in the USA, English sites and documents pervade the Internet. Statistical estimates suggest that three quarters of the pages on the World Wide Web are in English. However, only 5.4 per cent of the world's population have English as their mother tongue and only a 7 per cent of the world's population are proficient English speakers. So only an eighth of the world's population understands and speaks English.

International Data Corporation, Forrester Research and Allied Business Intelligence report as follows:

1. Over half of today's 147 million Internet users are non-English speakers. Within four years, they will be more than two thirds. Within two years, the non-US percentage of the e-commerce market will account for 46 percent of a $1.3 trillion market.

2. Users are four times more likely to purchase from a site that communicates in the customer's language.

3. The firm's Atlas II project predicts that within two years, over 50 percent of web users in Europe, 75 percent in South America, and 80 percent in Japan will make native language sites their preference.

4. Over half of US web sites do not internationalize their content. Forrester Research says that US e-commerce sites have to discard over half the orders they receive because they originated abroad and they cannot process the foreign information or lack of supply-chain mechanism.

5. In Latin America, the number of Internet users is predicted to increase to 75 million by 2005. Only trading in the region is estimated to amount to $72 billion US.

6. The number of Hispanic households in the US that own PCs increased by 42.3 percent between Q1 and Q4 of 2000. The overall rate of technology adoption by Hispanics in the US has been 80 percent over the last two years, as compared with 21 percent for the overall US market.

7. By 2005, China will be second to the US in number of Internet users.

8. By 2004, 50% of all online sales are expected to occur outside the US.

9. Although the web had predominantly been an English-centered medium, leading companies identify that 90% of their market outside the US is non-English speaking.

10. By the end of 2006 the worldwide professional translation market will account for $5.7 billion, and the automatic translation market will account for $117 million. The software and web localization markets will account for $3.5 billion and $3 billion, respectively.

11. Business to consumer sales will reach $108 billion by 2003 and business to business sales to reach over $1.3 trillion.

Despite the globalization and the predominance of English as an international language everybody speaks or understands:

The demand for linguistic and cultural adaptation of products, documents and web sites, and the trade of services internationally, it is stronger than ever and it is now one of the ways by which many people define their national and cultural identity in the world.

English dominance is set to decline in the Internet as its international access grows more and more and companies around the world put their information online and start to do e-business.

Point to remember:

Globalization and the Internet are just two of the changes which have dramatically altered the landscape of business and accelerated the rate and impact of change on corporations. Strategic planning has expanded to include quick access to markets, differentiated products and services, and better knowledge of the customer and the competition.

2.
DEFINITIONS

2.1. Globalization - the strategy

LISA, The localization Industry Standards Association defines globalization *as the business issues associated with taking a product global.*

Globalization is the strategic expansion of corporate content, assets and message across cultures and markets. It encompasses both, internationalization and localization.

Globalization is the strategy for worldwide presence of products and services.

Globalization has been associated with Internet companies, e-business and e-commerce. Therefore, most consumers believe that globalization is simply a multilingual web site, in other words, the e-globalization is enough for the world wide presence and the international business.

Everyone - a corporation, an established company or consultancy- who wants to have a global presence (should) face the same issue: being global is being local first.

Globalization is definitely more challenging for e-businesses as they exist online and they conduct all operations online. But having a multilingual web site is not enough. You will have to think of the logistics, distribution, payment, local phone numbers, customer support and training of your "global staff". Multinational corporations and well-established companies are dealing with all of this on a daily basis. They consist of their "international operations".

For example, how would a company globalize California raisin cookies? It would to: create a multilingual web site, register it in different countries and research engines, find distributors in local countries, educate them and offer customer services locally in the local language. This is the minimum requirement.

In other words, a simple web site is not enough.

Today, despite the increasing number of companies that claim themselves to be "globalization consultancies", multilingual web content management, localization and translation firms, there is NO ONE STOP SHOP as such. A company capable of delivering everything: from the globalization strategy to the local customer services does not yet exist.

At the time of this writing, mergers, acquisitions and strategic partnerships are being formed between different types of companies in this industry (e.g.: software localizers are merging with translation agencies, international registers etc) hoping to create one-stop shops.

Globalization remains a concept. As a planned strategy that works with the help of different vendors and suppliers, each one specializing in their fields.

2.2. What is internationalization? (abbreviation I18N)

What is internationalization? According to LISA, *it is the process of generalizing a product, so that it can handle multiple languages and cultural conventions without the need for redesign. For example, be sure that the application supports double byte characters so you can translate it into Chinese and Japanese.*

Internationalization involves making programs and their user interface easy to localize. A fully internationalized code will handle all types of character sets and display formats, and isolate language specific-programming data.

Thei Zervaki

Internationalization refers to the process of reengineering software so it can recognize and process any language. It also involves making changes in the code so the software can understand other potential differences such as multiple currencies and local date formats.

In other words, internationalization is the process of writing code that can be easily translated in other languages.

2.3. What is localization? (abbreviation L10N)

LISA (The localization Industry Standards Association) defines localization *as follows: the process in taking a product and making it linguistically and culturally appropriate to the target locale (country/region and language) where it will be used and sold. The term localization derives from the term locale, which is defined in the Webster dictionary as a place or a locality especially when viewed in relation to a particular event; a site; a scene. As a consequence, locale is a collection of standard settings, rules and data specific to a language and geographical region. If you want to translate a web site in German but all of your German speaking customers are from Switzerland, it will probably be a better idea to localize it for Switzerland (where the German spoken is a different locale to the German spoken in Germany).*

Other definitions from web sites:

Localization is the process of translating and adapting software, web sites and other products so that they are perceived as having been developed in the user's country. It requires intimate knowledge of cultural imperatives, technology, and industry standards.

Even if the definition is far too honest, it describes reality. Most of the time, web sites, products and software are localized in the headquarters of an organization (corporation or business). However, as the definition says, users believe that these products have been developed locally.

Localization requires a complete conversion from addressing one audience to addressing another entirely different one. Written language translation is coupled with necessary format changes, the creation of correct links and finally, the adoption of a vital sensitivity to cultural differences.

Localization refers to the process of translating and culturally adapting software user interfaces, web pages, help files, documentation, and other content for one specific language or locale.

In other words, it is not only the translation but also the cultural adaptation from one language and culture to another. It means tailoring products, software and web sites to match the language, customs and idioms of the target local market or country. The term is mainly used for web sites and software, but all other materials such as marketing brochures, press releases, manuals, training material and more, need to be localized for the world market.

2.4. Translation, your friend in the global market

Definitions from different linguistic books:

Translation is the expression in another language (or target language) of what has been expressed on another source language, preserving semantic and stylistic equivalents.

OR

Thei Zervaki

Translation is the replacement of a representation of a text in one language by a representation of an equivalent text in a second language.

Translation is understanding the source text in a language and then reproducing the same text in a target language. A good knowledge of the source language as well as the target together with cultural and stylistics references is necessary to deliver quality.

3.

TIPS FOR BUSINESSES

3.1. Do you need to localize?

Taking the priority that you want to have a global presence, you need to ask the following questions:

Do you need to localize your web site, your software or products? How will you find this out?

a. Do a SWOT analysis: what are your strengths, weaknesses, opportunities and threats as a company? See it in relation with your target markets and clients, countries of expansion and competitors.

b. What kind of business are you in? A corporation, e-business or a small traditional business looking for global expansion?

c. Identify your needs: how many languages do you want to localize?

d. Define which of your products need to be localized: your web site, your marketing material, training documentation, software or everything?

e. Investigate the market: benchmark with competitors.

f. Investigate your target markets: Europe, Asia, US or South America?

g. Do not forget the interior US market -Asians, Latinos, Europeans.

h. Analyze the cost in relation to the benefit: is it worth it?

11

3.2. For web site localization

Many companies notice considerable reductions in cost, mainly in printing and distribution, since a localized web site offers all information to customers, users and consumers. In addition, they can download PDF files and information. Many companies have experienced a lower number of customer support phone calls as well. However, this should not be taken for granted: many others, do not actually see any difference in cost from a localized web site.

Note to remember: most companies localize and translate their site and products because they want to sell more, in other words, they target a higher revenue.

If you decide that localization is something you really need, you need to proceed as follows:

1. Do you have a strategy when you localize/translate? (which countries/regions come first, how many languages, how do you go about it?)
2. How do you fund localization and translation costs?
3. Do your customers get involved in the process?
4. How will you organize your localization/translation needs?
5. How will you choose your vendor?

3.3. Explore your options

3.3.1. Localization needs organized in-house:

Advantages
1. A centralized approach.

2. You have control of everything.
3. It is easier to review.
4. There is a guarantee of quality.

Disadvantages
1. Cost effective.
2. It is time consuming to get organized. You will have to find the budget, then advertise to find the most competent people in the market, train them, and start working together.

Before you opt for it, ask: will you need permanent in-house translators or you will need them for a specific period of time or for just one specific project? If the answer is yes in the second case, then maybe you should choose a vendor.

3.3.2. Hiring a vendor

Hiring a vendor is not an easy task as there are many available in the market today. There are hundreds of localization and translation agencies in the market and selecting the best one for you will require some time and effort from your side.

Advantages

1. When you outsource, you don't do the job yourself, somebody else is taking care of it. Most localization companies are professional and they can guarantee quality assurance (QA).
2. Localization companies offer CAT solutions and translation databases. Web workflow systems are becoming popular so consistency in terminology and style is guaranteed.

3. Experience in similar projects. Referrals from previous clients can work as a proof.

Disadvantages

1. Bear in mind that vendors use freelance translators or subcontract translation agencies themselves, so the whole process "visits" different people. As a consequence, communication problems and delays in delivery can be an issue.
2. You do not have any control over production.
3. The cost may be prohibitive.

3.3.3. Using freelancers

Advantages

1. It can be more cost-effective than the other solutions.

Disadvantages

1. Time consuming. You have to follow the same process as hiring an in-house team.
2. It would be cheaper but more troublesome. Freelance translators are all over the world, you will have to screen, hire, commission, send material and brief them.
3. Lack of control. You may think you control the process but you don't and unless you can provide a sophisticated web workflow based engine, expect certain problems, in particular when many freelancers work on the same target language.

4. Lack of consistency and cohesion in terminology.

3.4. How to choose a vendor

a. If you decide to hire a vendor: ask for a proposal. This will be the basis for the selection of your vendor. Check their client list and references as well.

b. Ask for a translation test piece. Most of the times, it is free of charge. What to look at: understanding of source text, grammar, punctuation and spelling, terminology knowledge and consistency, style, presentation, overall impression.

c. Compare prices with other vendors/agencies/freelance translators.

d. Check their location: will the time difference be a problem if the vendor is located in a different continent?

e. Find out in detail what they offer and for what price. Do they offer translation databases, memory tools, XML, web workflow engines? And for what cost?

f. Is translation centralized or is done in local offices in the target language related country?

3.4.1. What to check for in particular

1. What services is the vendor offering?
2. What are their hours of operation?
3. What is their daily capacity?
4. What are their references?
5. Are their rates within 10-15% of median price and do they have an open and detailed price structure?
6. Do they have experience in similar localization projects?

7. Do they have the technical competence in the relevant operating environments?

8. Are they committed to good and frequent project related communication?

9. Do they have all the needed recourses to avoid delays?

10. Are they committed to quality and customer service through detailed quality processes and technology? And finally

11. Are they committed to your company as an ongoing account by using gained experience on previous projects through internal training?

3.4.2. Some other issues you will have to address:

a. Train the localization vendor and all people involved on the process for the localization project and on the products/software to be localized.

b. Be clear, specific and explicit.

c. Reduce bureaucracy.

d. Keep the vendor informed at all stages of the project.

e. Request price guarantees - in case the scope of the project changes.

f. Review pricing.

g. Set reasonable deadlines.

h. Be professional at all stages.

i. Work on your global English.

At the time of this writing, many companies are in the process of developing engines, intranets and software for web flow, project and client management solutions. Moreover, businesses are becoming more and more demanding and in a way, the sophisticated software and engines have been developed to meet their requests. However, before choosing such a vendor, check the cost, the real time needed for the training and the use of the service and if it is worth it. Sometimes sophisticated packages tend to be more expensive, time consuming and cumbersome than the traditional ways of doing business.

Note to remember

ASP solutions: are web translation repositories, where all vendors can share the information. They use workflow and management technologies that track down - route documents to the correct people automatically. A server application tracks down changes in the web site, sends out the content for localization and inserts it back at the site. So you can centralize and you decentralize at the same time.

3.5. Getting the budget

Do you have a separate budget for translation? Are you a marketing executive or production manager within your company and need a budget to localize? Does management know or does not care about it?

Translation and localization operations and teams are part of the marketing and communication divisions. Therefore, the budget needed will be credited from the communication's division budget. But how will you convince your manager or the CEO to fund your translation projects in 14 languages for example? What are you going to say?

Top management executives and CEOs in the US do not always realize the necessity of the localization as a concept and process. "I can watch CNN in English where I am in Moscow, what's the point of translation? I can speak English in Tokyo, do we really need to localize?" These are questions you might have to answer.

Executives and managers who want to localize, have two options:

1. Communicate your request to top management and then wait for them to decide if they can do it or not. If they give you the go-ahead, you will then have to find the most "affordable" vendor.

2. Show "numbers" to management: compare market potential and sales opportunities to convince them - more languages, more sales. Benchmark with your competitors. Present them with results of research companies regarding multilingual users of the Internet.

The choice is yours.

3.6. The structure of pricing for translation

The structure of pricing for translation is based on:

1. The language combinations.
2. The area of specialization.
3. Use or not of CAT tools.
4. The deadline.
5. The text format.

Plus the additional localization and project management costs.

Note to remember

Files to be translated should pass from the following people: Project manager, translator, reviewer (editor and/or proofreader), engineer, QA and then again to the project manager. In some localization companies, the account manager and the production manager are also involved.

3.7. Work on your English for global documentation

If you want to decrease the cost of localization within your organization, please do work on your English. You will need to show consistency, clarity in style and expression and be culturally sensitive.

Here are a few handy tips:

3.7.1. Use plain English and be clear in style

1. Use short and complete sentences in correct English.
2. Use questions and statements in positive terms.
3. Use relative pronouns.
4. Define abbreviations and acronyms (do not overuse).
5. Be unambiguous.
6. Use punctuation.
7. Do not overuse advanced terminology.

3.7.2. Be culturally neutral

1. Avoid metaphors, analogies and similes.
2. Use globally acceptable icons and symbols.

3. Avoid idioms and slang.

4. Do not use neologisms.

5. Avoid humor.

6. Be cautious with descriptions of people, cultures and civilizations.

4.

TIPS FOR TRANSLATION AGENCIES AND LOCALIZATION VENDORS

In the first example, it is a small company composed from 1 to 10 people. In the second, they are big stock exchange listed corporations. See the difference? However, the process of translating is the same in both cases. The localization company has added responsibilities - especially if it is software and web localization.

What localization vendors do?

They mainly deliver: translated, reformatted and linguistically reviewed hard copy and on-line technical documentation, web content and software.

4.1. General advice for all vendors

1. Be professional.
2. Screen translators before you decide to have them on your database.
3. Have translators in your data based on their specialization sectors, language combinations and availability.
4. Have in-house translators, who have knowledge of major languages.
5. Train translators!
6. Keep up-to-date: review new CAT products, newsletters and subscriptions.
7. Offer a translation test.
8. Send detailed proposals and quotes to potential clients.

9. Be competitive in the market.
10. Offer real multilingual solutions, not just simple translation - efficiency is more important than price.
11. Guarantee quality assurance.

4.2. The translation test piece

By offering a test piece you:

1. Test your in-house process.
2. Examine your quality of the translation offered.
3. See if you can meet deadlines.
4. Test your translation/localization knowledge.

When you do the test piece:

1. Use your "best" in the area of specialization vendors.
2. Always pay the vendors for the test piece.
3. Never charge the client, test pieces are free of charge.
4. Always use a second vendor as the reviewer.
5. Usually offer a 2,000 word file with a 3 days' turnaround.

Before you start, check the following:

1. Ask for reference material such as glossaries, web sites, guides, etc.
2. Know the target audience and readers.
3. Who is the assessor on behalf of the client?

4. What are their evaluation and selection criteria?
5. Do they test you in only one or more languages?
6. Have they ever used the same vendors/suppliers you use?

After the completion of the test piece:

1. Make a list of the difficulties and how they were solved.
2. Justify terminology and style used.
3. Make your recommendations to improve the production and delivery of the test piece.

4.3. How to choose translators for your agency/company

1. Advertise in specialized newsletters and publications, translation web sites, colleges and universities.
2. Evaluate sample translations or results of in-house translation tests.
3. Visit college recruitment fairs.
4. Keep in contact with Translation associations - they deliver lists of new members.
5. Use the web - there are plenty of translation sites with names, profiles and details of availability.

4.4. How to get clients

Something that becomes more and more difficult due to the tough competition between vendors.

1. Advertise your services in different industry publications - depending on your specialization area (if you are a top notch

agency in medical translation choose medical related publications).

2. Have a very concise and informative web site.
3. Visit trade shows, exhibitions, seminars and workshops.
4. Use your sales people.
5. Use networking- word of a mouth.

5.

THE PROCESS OF PROJECT MANAGEMENT IN TRANSLATION/LOCALIZATION INDUSTRIES

Notes for successful project managers and what businesses should know about!

1. Operating system: ask your client what operating system they are using for localized documents. Is it Windows 98 or 2000? What about Macs? Be clear about it as files created in latest versions of Microsoft Word, for example, can't be read in previous versions.

2. Software: linked to the operating system. Especially crucial for double-byte characters such as Japanese. If you client is a Japanese client, you should be able to reproduce your deliverables in the Japanese version. You also need to take into consideration that you are using an acceptable and standard version/package of the software of the target country. If not, your client in Japan would not be able to open and read files.

3. Word count: VERY IMPORTANT. Make sure the number of words is accurate. Be aware, however, that different tools/methods you use to word count have different results (Word, TRADOS, FrameMaker). Word for example will not count words separated by a slash as separate words. Agree with clients and translators from the beginning which method you are going to use to avoid pitfalls. Word count is a cost related issue that's why it is very important to clarify things from the start.

4. References/lexicals/glossaries: ask the client for all related references, literature and glossaries related to the product. If the client can't provide you with references, make sure that all material used is approved by the client as terminology should be respected and consistent. You will avoid having problems with reviewers as well. For example, some terms might be perfect in the central office of an organization or a company but local agencies might have a different opinion. Again, communication between you and your client is crucial.

5. Translation memory tools/language databases: does the client want you to use translation memory tools? This is considered to be very professional as it guarantees consistency and cohesion in terminology and increases productivity. However, it affects cost as the process becomes more expensive. In addition, as businesses are not translation literate, they are confused about machine translation and memory tools. It is up to you to clarify the differences.

6. Price: the price issue is a very complicated one. It is not only worked out by word count and markup as most of you know. You have to add costs for editing, proofreading, reviewing, and also shipping of hard copies or CDs if needed from the client.

7. Deliverables (file format/graphics): what format will your files be delivered in? In Word, PDF, txt or other? And what about graphics? Does the client want them localized as well? Clarify the different file formats to the clients and ask them to communicate to you exactly what they want. If they send HTML files instead of Word as you thought in the beginning, translators will ask for more money and will need more time. In addition, conversion from one format to another is time consuming, complicated and affects profitability.

8. QA: each translation should pass first from the translator and then from the reviewer (in very good cases, vendors use two reviewers, the proofreader and the editor).

9. Schedule: this is the result of the above and what makes a localization vendor/ project manager successful: deliver quality work at a reasonable price on time.

6.

WEB CONTENT MANAGEMENT (in relation with the marketing/localization or communications department)

Although document management controls the outer shell of documents, content management manages the pieces and chunks of information within. Content management offers the added functionality of reuse, structure and XML tagging. In addition, the writers reusing the information within a document are limitless.

There are three types of content (GRL) - in the localization process:

Global: content that will stay the same for all markets as history, logos, investor relations. You will have to translate it but do not need to localize as it is general information.

Regional: content relevant to a particular region or group of countries. That will include product information, marketing material, PR and communication material and the interface of the site. This content is written once and then localized for each country's language and culture.

Local: it is the locale specific. This content is written from the beginning for a particular market. That includes: local offices details, telephone numbers and contact names. Make sure that this content is updated on the site!

7.

COMPUTER AID TRANSLATION (CAT)

CAT is the broadest term used to describe an area of computer technology applications that automates or assists the act of translating a text from the source language to the target language.

There are three major categories of these tools currently available in the market:

7.1. Machine Translation

MACHINE TRANSLATION: it is a software developed to rearrange or decode text from one natural language to another. Based on advanced computational linguistic analysis MT engines process source documents linguistically to create a new document into the target language.

The benefits from MT products depend on a number of factors including the source document and their effectiveness can be impaired if the source document has:

- Typographic errors
- Grammatical errors
- Complex sentence structure
- Jargon
- Stylistic complexity
- Limited dictionaries developed in the MT product
- Advanced terminology

They can provide benefits in three ways:

a. For gisting where and when the user would like to understand the general meaning.
b. For screening large amounts of documents in order to identify what warrant more accurate human translation.
c. For conveying simple instructions or non-complex information sent with the original source text.

Language combinations availability.
MT products are available in a limited set of language combinations. This is because the linguistic rules for analysis and parsing of the source text vary by language. In addition, the market needs determine the number of language combinations currently available.

7.2. Machine Assisted Human Translation (MAHT)

a. Translation memory: The TM database stores previously translated sentences, building up a large repository of source text and foreign language equivalents over time. With the assistance of "fuzzy matching" functionality, the system also recognizes similar, not just identical, translation matches.
b. Translator's workbench: they help the translator in processing and managing the project. That includes word count, sizing, costing, format converters, alignment tools to create memories from previous translations.

BENEFITS:

1. Better translation consistency, particularly valuable when many translators are involved.
2. Reduction of total time of translation up to 50%.
3. Reduction of total translation costs of 15% to 30%.
4. Reduced time-to-market time for localization of products.
5. Particularly savvy when translating repetitive texts such as standardized forms, operating manuals, contracts, product updates and successive versions of other texts.

7.3. Terminology managers

Translating terminology is a tedious task of researching the terms used in high specialized documents such as medical, legal, engineering and finding their translations.

Terminology managers provide key functions in this task:

a. They create a terminology repository as they serve as a collection point for gathering and storing source and target terminology for later use and re-use in the translation process. However, the techniques or tools used for storing and retrieving terms can vary by product.

b. You can use them to look up a term rapidly. Most terminology managers available map source to target terminology in one-to-one correspondence. The most sophisticated can store them based on concept.

c. You have automated terminology insertion. Term managers will insert the translate term into the target document without the need to re-type or cut and paste.

8.

ONLINE TRANSLATION SERVICES

Many translation companies, translation portals and other related sites offer online translation services. These can be:

1. Online purchase of translation services. You can order your translation online by uploading your documents, specifying the language pairs and paying by credit card. The translation is done by professional translators and is sent to you when ready.

2. Online Machine translation. MT software integrated by the translation portal. It is usually free and real time. You can either translate a document, a web site or email. In most cases, you have a draft translation document or "gisting" of your source documents.

MT software used online can be useful for and allow the following:

- Text "gisting"
- Email translation
- Web page translation
- Search translation

9.

TIPS FOR LANGUAGE ISSUES: WHAT TO LOOK FOR

1. Word order varies between languages.
2. Word delimiters are non-existent in certain oriental languages (Thai, Japanese).
3. Capitalization: oriental languages often do not have capitalization, some languages allow accented capitals.
4. Hyphenation.
5. Spelling and grammar.
6. Punctuation conventions (question mark in Spanish for example).

10.

TIPS FOR CROSS-CULTURAL AND LOCALIZATION ISSUES: A FEW EXAMPLES

Consider and be sensitive to social, religious and political conventions at all times.

The basic issues you have to deal with are:

Payment/Currency: prices should be expressed in local currencies - don't forget the exchange rate with dollar.

Numbers representations differ in separators: decimal separator, thousands separators, list separators.

Time zones: Dates must be in the right format and sequence (in Europe put the day first and then the month). Find out the different time zones and calendars (lunar, Gregorian).

Also, **weights and measures** should be familiar.

Content: It includes colors, images and graphics. Black is seen as the sombre color of mourning in most countries but it is a lucky color for Chinese. A German ad for a bank shows mice sitting on some coins! Because mice is a slang word for money in German. This will have to be changed when translated.

The famous X in a box - a common technique on web pages for selecting items from a list. In Korea and Switzerland this means that the item should be excluded rather included. Or the picture of the US mailbox as the symbol for e-mail may be confusing to a European or

Asian. Or pointing fingers have different socially connotations in different cultures. Jokes and humor can be used but with caution.

General cultural and religious issues:

1. Europeans: more difficult to work with as each country has different habits, ethics and customs.
2. Muslims: special language requirements as well. Avoid referring to Christmas, Easter and other religious dates. Find out about Muslim major events. Remember that alcohol and pork are not allowed.
3. Hebrews: avoid referring to Christmas, Easter and other religious dates. Find out about Jewish major events. Special food requirements should be included, especially if you are in the food industry business.

Customer support: even if the 1-800 is a free number in the USA, this does not mean is free in other countries. Find out about free numbers locally and regionally.

11.
TIPS FOR TRANSLATORS/LINGUISTS

11.1. Definitions

Linguists should:

1. Know at least one foreign language.
2. Master their first/mother tongue.
3. Know the linguistic theories.
4. Be able to apply different aspects of Linguistic theory in at least one language.
5. Have knowledge of different levels of the language system.
6. Have been trained in at least one sector of Linguistics.
7. Be able to do research independently in the use of language.
8. Understand the communication problems in every day life.
9. Be able to interpret the language values in the social context.
10. Be able to identify and classify problems in textual and communication context.

Translators should:

1. Master their first/mother or target language.
2. Know at least one foreign language.
3. Have excellent writing skills in the first/target language.
4. Have excellent knowledge of international and current affairs.

5. Keep themselves up-to-date in different aspects of technology, politics, economy, medicine.
6. Have specialization in one particular industry.
7. Have passive knowledge of different languages.
8. Be familiar with CAT products and software packages.
9. Be commercially oriented.

A translator should deal with:

- Context
- Terminology
- Style
- Language: spelling, punctuation

11.2. Studies

A University degree in Languages/Linguistics and/or Translation is a must these days. Many translators have a degree in Languages and then go for a Masters in Translation.

If you have a degree in a different discipline and you want to get in the translation business, a Masters degree will help you out.

Translation Schools graduates have different options.

Option 1: get into the translation/localization business. Mother or first language will determine your career path. Generally speaking, translators with strong mother or first languages as French, German, Spanish, Chinese and Japanese (except for English) will have more job options and opportunities mainly because there is a great demand for translation in these languages. They can work in-house or freelance for major localization companies and for smaller translation agencies. The country of residence will also determine their job opportunities. It is easier to find a job as an in-house or freelance translator in your native country as your language skills will be very much appreciated. Working abroad is also a good path but it might be more difficult (often due to employment legislation).

Moreover, get specialized in one particular area depending on your interests. Medical, legal, financial or IT are the "hot" sectors.

Option 2: use language and linguistic knowledge and skills to do something completely different in sectors where languages are very appreciated and needed. These sectors can be identified as: international banking and investing, media, politics and diplomacy, international management and commerce. Additional qualifications in the sector of choice as Masters, Postgraduate diplomas or industry accreditation certificates will be very helpful for future career choices.

More tips:

- Literary translation pays well, if you become experienced and you are a well- established translator in the market.
- Keep updated in your field and industry
- Be familiar with CAT products
- Check your progress: do you want a vertical or parallel promotion? Do you want to become a Project manager or add more languages? Do you want to write books on translation, to get invitations to conferences to talk about translators or to project manage? If you want to add more languages, investigate the market of your country or your mother tongue related. Will Swahili be useful for you if you target language

is Swedish? Or you should go for Chinese, German or Spanish instead?

11.3. Going freelance

1. The business of translation: is of great demand but competitive. Bear in mind your language combinations and your first/target language. If you translate into German and your source languages are Chinese and French, you will probably have a lot of potential to make good money!

2. Business plan: Write down your minimal objectives of the year (the money you will need for your initial investment and to stay on the market). Then set higher goals for the years to come. Finally, have a dream plan ready (you want to move to the Caribbean and hire other freelancers to work for you!).

3. Market your services/find clients: as a freelancer, you have the advantage to work with both agencies and individual clients. Have your web site, business cards and advertise in relevant newsletters.

4. Have the necessary equipment: PC, Internet connection, modem, telephone, fax. Software and CAT products. Dictionaries, reference books.

5. Train: keep up-to-date in your areas of specialization. Read. Subscribe to magazines. Visit conferences, do seminars and workshops.

6. Pricing: try to be competitive but do not under price yourself either.

7. Quality assurance: always check your finished translations. Even better, hire an editor to review it before you hand it in.

8. Plans for the future: learn a new language. Specialize in a new area. Decide which direction you want to go: create your

own agency? Start offering interpretation as well? Or maybe language training and cross-cultural consultancy?

12.

THE FUTURE OF LOCALIZATION

A few months ago, linguistic magazines predicted that the future of localization will be mostly web-based. Now, we currently "live" the future as integrated web-based software applications enable clients to create, localize, manage, warehouse, reuse and distribute information tailored for global and local needs. Major localization vendors offer these solutions and many more are currently developing more sophisticated products.

More predictions for the future of the industry?

Networks of translators and localization tools will work together into a small number of database repositories of content located at customer sites or distributed regionally especially for user assistance material (vendors, publishers and document processing)

Moreover, localization companies are expanding in different directions: some offer training, call centers and support services. Others go towards consulting, design and ASP.

We also see and we will see many partnerships and strategic alliances in the years to come between corporations, localization companies, globalization companies and management consultancies.

13.

WHAT IS THE FUTURE FOR THE ENGLISH LANGUAGE?

A typical English speaker believes that the language is becoming increasingly simplified, even as English as a whole grows more complex.

English is going to continue to become simpler in structure and the choice of vocabulary. The language is changing to meet the needs of its users. These users are scientists, researchers, scholars, pilots, radio officers, non-native Internet users, air-traffic controllers and English language broadcasters who have to use special vocabulary and simplified structure to enhance non traditional kinds of communication with non-native speakers.

Moreover, computers and the Internet were invented in the United States and have remained US-centric since then. Even if the dominance of English in the Internet is loosening, English will be the founding and default language of PCs and the Internet. However, wireless Internet becomes a new territory and was not invented in any country. Wireless Internet is not US-born. This might have an effect on English language in the years to come.

What is the Plain English Network?

The Plain English Network is a government-wide group of volunteers working to improve communications from the federal government to the public. Their web site contains lots of resources to help writers achieve the goal of clear communication.

Remember these three principles:

- Use reader-oriented writing. Write for your customers, not for other government employees.

- Use natural expression. To the extent possible, write as you would speak. Write with commonly used words in the way that they are commonly used.

- Make your document visually appealing. Present your text in a way that highlights the main points you want to communicate.

The following list of companies, web sites, online machine translation portals, translation associations and research engines are far from being a very detailed list of the industry. This is a comprehensive and useful list with the very basic names you need: to localize a web site, find a translation association in Belgium or buy an online dictionary to practice your favourite language.

In the near future, localization companies are looking to form strategic partnerships with globalization consultancies, web content management firms and software developers to create one-stop shops to meet all the demands of customers. This is where the industry is going. One-stop shops offer translation and localization services to web workflow management and online MT portals.

1.
LOCALIZATION COMPANIES

THE BIG FIVE

ALPNET

http://www.alpnet.com: major localization, translation and multilingual content management public company. Alpnet uses InfoCycle, a new multilingual information management model that identifies solutions and efficiencies upstream at the information creation stage, where they can be planned and implemented. Partners with Chrystal software, a XML content management software provider. ALPNET has been acquired by SDL in January 2002.

BERLITZINET

http://www.berlitzglobalnet.com: Berlitz GlobalNET, the translation services subsidiary of Berlitz, is the world's largest supplier of translation, localization and interpretation services with production and management facilities in 20 countries. Berlitz GlobalNET offers full production capabilities including eCommerce translation, software localization, globalization, and project management, as well as simultaneous and consecutive interpretation services.

BOWNEGLOBAL

http://www.bowneglobal.com: Bowne's global team delivers strategy consulting, technical communication, product localization and multi-language web content creation. Bowne Global Solutions and GlobalSight Corp. announced a strategic alliance designed to help global companies successfully compete on the multilingual Internet. In addition, Bowne Global together with Oracle Worldwide Product Translation group deliver the complete set of Technology Based Training courses in five major languages. Bowne Global acquired Mendez in October 2001.

LIONBRIDGE

http://www.lionbridge.com: Lionbridge (Nasdaq: LIOX) integrates technology, translation, and consulting to help clients create and maintain information-based products and services for multiple cultural, linguistic, technical, and business targets. It's one of the largest localization companies with offices worldwide.

SDL

http://www.sdlintl.com: a localization and multilingual content management provider. They develop and use SDLWebFlow, an optional integration with SDL International's Enterprise Translation Server that enables translations in real-time. This translation capability allows SDLWebFlow 3.0 to provide instant multilingual translations to increase the cost-effectiveness and breadth of user applications delivered by SDLWebFlow.

ABLE INTERNATIONAL

http://www.ableintl.com: translation and localization solutions for global markets. ABLE has developed proprietary workflow technology tools that also provide with translation portal-like capabilities - AJAX, which stands for ABLE's Job Automation exchange software.

ARCHITEXT

http://www.architext-usa.com: a translation and localization services provider. ArchiText invented *A*BREVE, a system that produces streamlined translation-ready source materials.

ETRANSLATE.COM

http://www.etranslate.com: specialising in web localization. It uses the GlobalWeb solution which is supported by its proprietary technology, GlobalLink. GlobalLink is a multilingual content management software that streamlines the localization process. ULTRA is a suite of applications to automate, extend, and optimize the translation and localization process.

INTERSOLINC

http://www.intersolinc.com: localization and translation solutions together with web design and development of multilingual web sites.

IO-TEK

http://www.io-tek.com: IO-TEK is a multicultural Application Service Provider (ASP) focused on the development of proprietary software applications and delivery of strategic services to address an enterprise's globalization and cultural localization needs.

LEXFUSION

http://www.lexfusion.com: Translation and Localization company. LexFusion is powered by Prolyphic, an enterprise-wide collaborative solution that centralizes all of your company's globalization and localization projects, resources and assets.

RUBRIC

http://www.rubric.com: One of the specialists in the localization process, Rubric focuses on streamlining the localization process by developing and using the Streamliner localization methodology. It reduces time-to-market, improves quality assurance while using expertise in translation, engineering and process management.

SIMULTRANS

http://www.simultrans.com: Simultrans offers customised solutions for clients by providing project management, linguistic, localization engineering and multilingual services all over the world. They have recently formalized their partnership with Alchemy software, one of the industry's primary provider of software translation tools.

STAR

http://www.star-usa.net: a localization company that also develops CAT products and a web flow system called StarTrans. StarTrans is a translation workflow system relying on a Transit translation server for translation memory features. The system is designed to monitor the flow of documents from the end of the authoring process to the final version of the translation.

THE LANGUAGE TECHNOLOGY CENTRE

http://www.langtech.co.uk: provides translation, localization and consulting. In addition, the center developed the LTC Organiser is a unique and innovative business process management and workflow control software system, which supports and facilitates multilingual translation projects. It is therefore of considerable use to translation companies worldwide.

WELOCALIZE

http://www.welocalize.com: a globalization services company offering clients multilanguage business consulting and localization solutions. The company has developed XTEND, a scaleable, web-enabled, enterprise wide workflow system for managing multi-language web sites and software localization projects. The XTEND suite is an integrated family of products including the XTEND Technology Kit (xTK) for text extraction and translation memory database preparation, and the XTEND Client Interface (xCI) for real-time project tracking via any browser.

2.

LOCALIZATION SPECIALISTS IN RARE LANGUAGES

LOGRUS

http://www.logrus.ru: specializes in Russian

LOMAC

http://www.lomac.net: for Central and Eastern European languages

SKANDISSYSTEM

http://www.skandissystems.com: Asian languages

TEKTRANSLATION

http://www.tektrans.com: a translation and localization services provider based in Madrid

3.

WORKFLOW AND PROCESS MANAGEMENT

ILANGUA.CO.UK

http://www.ilangua.com: TransMC is the re-brandable iLangua.com product allowing companies to establish e-procurement infrastructure that extends through to their client's intranet. TransMC represents a collection of Internet and wireless technologies that connect Translation Companies, their Clients and their Freelance Translators to improve communication and quality whilst reducing costs.

PROLYPHIC

http://www.prolyphic.com: Prolyphic is an industry-first web and browser based solution that provides workflow and project management, file analysis, and advanced translation memory tools.

STAR

http://www.star-usa.net: They developed StarTrans. StarTrans is a translation workflow system relying on a Transit translation server for translation memory features. The system is designed to monitor the flow of documents from the end of the authoring process to the final version of the translation. The translation workflow solution is customized based on the customers specific needs.

THE LANGUAGE TECHNOLOGY CENTRE

http://www.langtech.co.uk: the center developed the LTC Organiser is a unique and innovative business process management and workflow control software system, which supports and facilitates multilingual translation projects.

4.

GLOBALIZATION STRATEGY CONSULTANTS AND SERVICE PROVIDERS FOR E-BUSINESS AND B2B

GLOBALSIGHT

http://www.globalsight.com: provider of software and services for e-business globalization. GlobalSight System3 is a globalization server application that streamlines the process of developing multiple locale-specific sites to reach online customers in markets around the world. They offer strategy, products and services.

IDIOM

http://www.idiominc.com: another provider of services for e-business globalization. Their software, Worldserver, a web infrastructure software for enterprise globalization that embraces multiple countries, sites, languages, cultures and business practices while leveraging your existing web architectures, web content and other enterprise systems.

UNISCAPE

http://www.uniscape.com: Uniscape enables organizations to accelerate e-business globalization initiatives and effectively update global content through an infrastructure that manages how web content and resources are related and shared across multiple sites. The comprehensive solution includes a set of world-class globalization services delivered via our Global Enablement Methodology (G.E.M.) and the Uniscape Globalization Infrastructure (Uniscape GI), a technology platform that supports online e-business expansion across linguistic, cultural and national boundaries.

VISTATEC

http://www.vistaTec.ie: a globalization service provider to e-businesses, traditional businesses, software publishers and e-trading sites. Services include consulting and strategy, multilingual web development and account management.

5.

DOMAIN NAMES REGISTRATION

1GLOBALPLACE

http://www.1globalplace.com: is the one stop resource for e-commerce enterprises looking to expand into foreign markets and manage global assets. They provide global domain registration and management in over 115 countries and domain local presence qualification services.

I- DNS.NET

http://www.i-DNS.net: a multilingual internet solution provider.

REGISTRARS.COM

http://www.registrars.com: multilingual domain name registration. The first languages offered are Chinese, Korean and Japanese.

VERISIGN (Nasdaq: VRSN)

http://www.verisign.com: a provider of infrastructure services to web sites, electronic commerce service providers and individuals. Their products include: web site trust services, payment processing, global registry services, secure email, web authoring and web identity.

6.

WEB CONTENT MANAGEMENT

GLIDES

http://www.glides.com: an Internet infrastructure developer focuses its resources on building core technology for complex problems with web site globalization. Unisite, offers an easy-to-use solution for managing the development, deployment and maintenance of dynamic and multilingual web sites.

LANGUAGE AUTOMATION

http://www.lai.com: Their product, the WebPlexer system is a combination of integrated software modules and customizable translation services that work together to simplify the development, operation, translation and maintenance of a multilingual web site.

TRIDION

http://www.tridion.com: a web content management provider. Tridion DialogServer is a native-XML based enterprise software platform for global web content management that offers XML-based content lifecycle management, personalised content delivery and multi-channel publishing.

7.

CAT DEVELOPERS/ COMPANIES (MACHINE TRANSLATION, MEMORY TOOLS AND TERMINOLOGY MANAGERS)

ALCHEMY SOFTWARE

http://www.alchemysoftware.ie: developer of Alchemy Catalyst, the world's first integrated localization environment. Alchemy CATALYST technology is designed to boost the efficiency and quality of globalizing software products and is used by over 200 software development companies worldwide. Alchemy CATALYST is used by translators, software engineers, quality assurance specialists and project managers and is referred to as the Gold Standard in Localization.

ALIS

http://www.alis.com: developer of Gist-In-Time is a powerful, server-based language comprehension solution that lets you Auto-Translate documents into your own language. A gist is a computer-generated translation, instantly delivering the essential meaning of an electronic text written in a language foreign to the reader.

ATRIL

http://www.atril.com: A CAT developer company. They developed Déjà Vu, one of the most powerful and customisable CAT systems.

EPI-USE Systems

http://lexica.epiuse.co.za/CyberTrans.html: The EPI-USE Group is a world-class software and services business, with a strong global presence. CyberTrans is an online text & document translation system which allows you to translate text into a number of different languages. We are specialists who give guidance in the application of information technology in the local and international markets. Lexica, TRANSLATOR and Glossit form the basis of our natural language products and services. This range of products makes us the leading natural language processing experts in South Africa.

LANGUAGE ENGINEERING CORPORATION

http://www.lec.com/about/frame.html: LogoVista Translation model is one of the MT products. By using it, a vendor can create a translation system for a particular language pair and automatically have it used for translation of documents, Internet pages, etc. Similarly, a vendor can create a new use for translations, such as an e-mail translator, and immediately have access to translations in a wide variety of languages. Cooperation between components developed by different vendors becomes automatic, without the need for complex cross-licensing agreements.

LERNOUT AND HAUSPIE

http://www.lhsl.com: Power Translator Pro. L&H Power Translator Pro integrates into today's popular word processors (such as Microsoft Word 2000 and Corel WordPerfect) and popular e-mail programs, all you need to do is type and translate. You can use the Web Translator feature if you want to translate your web site.

LINGUATEC

http://www.linguatec.de: translation software and online translation providers and developers. Their products include: Personal translator PT 2001 and the e-translator server for up to 200 characters. Online dictionaries are also provided.

MENDEZ

http://www.mendez.com: except for traditional translation services, Mendez develops CAT products. The most famous is iTranslator: a product family that combines machine translation technology with human translation capabilities in a way that appears seamless to the end-user. Mendez offers integrated translation capabilities into Microsoft Word 2002 and office XP and via the Microsoft Office eServices web site. Mendez has been acquired by Bowne Global in October 2001.

MULTICORPORA

http://www.multicorpora.com: a CAT developer. MultiTrans is MultiCorpora's toolbox for translators and large organizations that perform translation. It allows for the creation and management of multilingual terminology data banks and for quick language-paired reference documents lookups. DoubleVue is an editing tool for translators and editors.

REVERSO

http://www.reverso.net: a translation software company. Products include: ReversoPro, ReversoPerso and Reverso Express. This software is used by Softissimo, a French portal for online translation of web sites and emails.

SALHR

http://www.sakhr.com: specializing in Arabic, they develop CAT tools, NLP software, OCR products and reading machines.

STAR

http://www.star-usa.net: a localization company that also develops CAT products. Transit and TermStar, the translation memory tool and terminology management tool are boxed solutions that you can purchase and use without any customisation.

SYSTRANSOFT

http://www.systransoft.com: the first machine translation software, SYSTRAN, with a wide platform of services and products ranging from software packages to on-line translation services using the web. It can translate directly from Ms Office, Outlook, Netscape or Internet explorer.

TRADOS

http://www.trados.com: The pioneer in Translation memory tool and terminology management developer. Most large and small translation and localization companies use Trados products. Trados Translation solution consists of Translator's workbench and WinAlign. MultiTerm is the software used for terminology management.

TRANSLATION EXPERTS LIMITED

http://www.tranexp.com: They have been developing natural language translation software and dictionaries. InterTran, MobileTran, NeuroTran and WordTran are all Machine Translation products translating documents, web sites and email messages.

TRANSLATIONWAVE (OTCBB: GTVCF)

http://www.translationwave.com: TranslationWave is a globalization company that transforms the Internet into a truly universal platform of communication. Translation: real-time email, database, PC-based software applications, text, chat room and web site.

8.

SPEECH RECOGNITION/TEXT-TO-SPEECH SOFTWARE

All major corporations have divisions that specialize in Speech technology and Natural language processing. For more information, visit their web sites.

IBM

http://www-4.ibm.com/software/speech: ViaVoice.

LERNOUT AND HAUSPIE

http://www.lhsl.com: Voice Xpress and Dragon NaturallySpeaking.

LINGUATECH

http://www.linguatec.de: ViaVoice pro.

NUANCE

http://www.nuance.com: Nuance 7.0, Verifier 2.0, Voyager, Vocalizer and Voice Web server.

OKI

http://www.oki.com/jp: SMARTTALK 3.0

SPEECHWORKS

http://www.speechworks.com: SpeechWorks 6, SpeechSite, Speechify, ETI-Eloquence.

9.

ONLINE MACHINE TRANSLATION COMPANIES AND DEVELOPERS FOR WEB SITES, EMAIL AND BROWSERS.

CHECK WEB SITES FOR ALL AVAILABLE LANGUAGE COMBINATIONS!

AMIKAI

http://www.amikai.com: Amikai is a leading Application Service Provider specializing in real-time, multilingual translation applications for the Internet. Products include AmiWeb, AmiChat, Amimail, Amitext. Their ready-to-use products are designed specifically for portals, ISPs, and community sites that have an international user base.

FREETRANSLATION.COM

http://www.freetranslation.com: an online free real time translation service/portal. You can have a real time web site translation and text translation. A division of SDLint.

ITRANSLATORONLINE.COM

http://www.itranslatoronline.com: A division of Mendez translations. Users can choose free machine translation for gist quality translations on the fly as well as the premium translation service, an on line human translation service with a quick turnaround time. The service is based on the iTranslator product family developed by Mendez.

LOGOMEDIA.NET

http://www.logomedia.net: LogoMedia is the premier source for quality, affordable language translation via the Internet and on the desktop. The company provides both automatic and human translation of documents, web sites, e-mails and more, to/from English and the major European and Asian languages.

SYSTRAN

http://www.systransoft.com: you can get draft translations of short paragraphs or even your web sites.

TRANSLATION EXPERTS LIMITED

http://www.tranexp.com: InterTran, short for Internet Translator, is a free web translation service that can translate single words, phrases, sentences and entire web pages between 767 language pairs. They have also developed MobileTran, for mobile telephones and WAP as well.

TRANSLATION.NET

http://www.translation.net: Translation.net offers a variety of professional translation and localization services. It directly connects you to Systranlink site for online MT.

TRANSLATIONS.COM

http://www.translations.com: a provider of enterprise translation solutions. It offers on line MT translations for short texts and web sites.

WORLDLINGO

http://www.worldlingo.com. Except for traditional translation and localization services, worldlingo.com offers online machine translation of web sites and documents, real time email translation and the Browser translation service, an instant MT translation (gisting) of web sites links. Microsoft offers Worldlingo translation services on its web site.

10.

ELECTRONIC DICTIONARIES AND MULTILINGUAL SOFTWARE DEVELOPERS (SPELLERS, DICTIONARIES, THESAURUS)

ECTACO

http://www.ectaco.com

POLDERLAND

http://www.polderland.nl

SMART LINK

http://www.smartlinkcorp.com

IS ILANGUAGE A ONE-STOP SHOP?

http://www.ilanguage.com: e-Business translation, web localization, globalization services and solutions. Their products include: Global eBiz™ package for globalization, Global eBuild™ for Content Management and Global CRM™ for worldwide Customer Relationship Management. In addition, ilanguage offers multimedia services aiming at delivering audio and video translations to handle the saturation of rich media content on the Internet.

ILANGUAGE is a one-stop shop because it formed partnerships with globalization companies, therefore, it can offer global solutions together with multilingual content management and translation services.

11.

PORTALS USING ONLINE MACHINE TRANSLATION

ALTAVISTA.COM

http://www.altavista.com Uses Systran software for its online services, called Babel Fish.

SIMPATICO.CA

http://www.simpatico.ca uses Alis Gist-In-Time machine translation software for real time translation as well as professional human translation on line—only the French site.

SOFTISSIMO

http://www.softissimo.com: French portal offering online machine translation on the fly using Reverso software.

12.

LANGUAGE RESELLERS AND RESOURCES OF PRODUCTS

LANGUAGEPARTNERS

http://www.languagepartners.com: Language   Partners International, Inc (LPI) provides translation management software and consulting services. They distribute CAT and localization tools: Deja vue, a translation memory tool, Alchemist Catalyst, the world's first integrated localization environment, Systran's MT products and Transcend natural language translator and project MT.

TRANSPARENT

http://www.transparent.com: they sell language learning packages and MT translation software—Easy Translator.

WORLDLANGUAGE

http://www.worldlanguage.com: everything you need!

THE INTERNET CORPORATION FOR ASSIGNED NAMES AND NUMBERS

http://www.icann.org

13.
ON-LINE WORK PLACES FOR TRANSLATORS

http://www.aquarius.net
http://www.proz.com
http://www.translationzone.com

14.

MAJOR TRANSLATION COMPANIES/AGENCIES

ADAMS TRANSLATION SERVICES

http://www.adamstrans.com

EXCEL TRANSLATIONS

http://www.yourtranslationpartner.com

FOREIGN EXCHANGE TRANSLATIONS

http://www.fxtrans.com

GLOBAL LANGUAGE SOLUTIONS

http://www.globallanguages.com

GLOBALVISION INTERNATIONAL

http://www.globalvis.com

INTERPRO TRANSLATION SOLUTIONS

http://www.interproinc.com

ISPEAK

http://www.ispeak.net

IVERSON LANGUAGE ASSOCIATES

http://www.iversonlang.com

JLS LANGUAGE CORPORATION
http://www.jls.com

LFI Worldwide
http://www.lfiww.com

LINGO SYSTEMS
http://www.lingosys.com

LUZ
http://www.luz.com

NETWORKOMNI
http://www.networkomni.com

PRAETORIUS NORTH AMERICA
http://www.praetorius.com

PRESTIGE NETWORK
http://www.prestigenetwork.com

RALPH MCELROY TRANSLATION COMPANY
http://www.mcelroytranslation.com

RWS Group
http://www.translate.com

SH3

http://www.sh3.com

VIALANGUAGE

http://www.vialanguage.com

15.
LOCALIZATION ASSOCIATIONS AND ORGANIZATIONS

Localization Industry Standards Association (LISA)
http://www.lisa.org

Professional Association for Localization (PAL)
http://www.PAL10n.org

The Language Technology Research Center
http://www.languagetech.com

The Localization Institute
http://www.localizationinstitute.com

The Localization Research Centre (LRC)
http://lrc.csis.ul.ie

The Silicon Valley Localization Forum
http://www.tgpconsulting.com

16.

MACHINE TRANSLATION RESOURCES AND SITES

European Machine Translation Association
http://www.lim.nl/eamt/

Association for Machine Translation in Americas
http://www.isi.edu/natural-language/organizations/AMTA.html

Asia-Pacific Association for Machine Translation
http://it.jeita.or.jp/aamt/

International Association for Machine Translation
http://www.isi.edu/natural-language/organizations/IAMT-bylaws.html

Thei Zervaki

17.
SITES FOR COMPUTATIONAL LINGUISTICS AND NLP

Association for Computational Linguistics
http://www.aclweb.org/

18.
LANGUAGE RESOURCES

European Language Resources Association
http://www.icp.inpg.fr/ELRA/

Plain English Network
http://www.plainlanguage.gov

The Linguistic Data consortium
http://www.ldc.upenn.edu/

The Translation Reference Center
http://www.transref.org

19.
PUBLICATIONS/NEWSLETTERS

Language International

http://www.language-international.com

Multilingual Computing

http://www.multilingual.com

20.
BOOKS

A practical guide to Localization by Bert Esselink.

Translating into Success: cutting-edge strategies for going multilingual in a global age by Robert C. Sprung.

Web Globalization: Write Once, Deploy Worldwide by Thomas Dwyer.

21.
UNIVERSITIES AND COLLEGES OFFERING DEGREES OR COURSES IN LOCALIZATION

AUSTIN COMMUNITY COLLEGE

http://www2.austin.cc.tx.us/taltaner

UNIVERSITY OF WASHINGTON

http://courses.washington.edu/softloc

22.
ETIQUETTE

PACIFIC RIM PROTOCOL
http://www.pacificrimprotocol.com

PROTOCOL CONSULTANTS INTERNATIONAL
http://www.protocolconsultants.com

THE PROTOCOL SCHOOL OF PALM BEACH
http://www.etiquetteexpert.com

THE PROTOCOL SCHOOL OF WASHINGTON
http://www.psow.com

23.
INTERCULTURAL MANAGEMENT AND TRAINING

BERLITZ
http://www.berlitz.com/cross_cultural/cross_cultural.html

CENDANT INTERCULTURAL
http://www.cendantintercultural.com

COGHILL AND BEERY
http://www.coghillbeery.com

IOR GLOBAL SERVICES
http://www.iorworld.com

24.

ONLINE CROSS-CULTURAL RESOURCES

AMANDA.COM
http//:www.amanda.com

CULTURESAVVY.COM
http//:www.culturesavvy.com

DIVERSOPHY.COM
http//:www.diversophy.com

WEB OF CULTURE
http//:www.webofculture.com

25.

USEFUL SITES FOR TRANSLATORS

A translation journal

http://www.accurapid.com/journal/links.htm

Post and find jobs on line with:

http://www.aquarius.net

Multilingual portal and language related information, chat rooms and courses

http://www.language9.com

All you need: associations, schools, magazines, dictionaries and products!

http://www.rahul.net/lai/companion.html

26.

USEFUL SITES FOR LINGUISTS

The Linguistic Society of America: information about Linguistics, linguistic programs, jobs, seminars and publications.

http://www.lsadc.org/

Information about linguistics, linguistic associations, magazines, translation, language instruction.

http://www.omnilex.com

Specifically targeted linguists in academia and research, with jobs, research papers and many other.

http://linguistlist.org

Linguistic Enterprises is a non-profit site that aims to help academically trained linguists find private sector employment. Useful tips for linguists, job offers and a mentoring scheme are available on the site.

http://web.gc.cuny.edu/dept/lingu/enter/toc2.htm

27.

EUROPEAN UNION SPONSORED SITES RELATED TO LANGUAGE TECHNOLOGY

HLT - Human Language Technology web site

HLTCentral web site was established as an online information resource of human language technologies and related topics of interest to the HLT community at large. It covers news, R&D, technological and business developments in the areas of speech, language, multilinguality, automatic translation, localization and related areas. It has a unique European perspective with a broad view of HLT news and developments worldwide.

http://www.hltcentral.org/htmlengine.shtml?id=55

ELSNET (The European Network of Excellence in Human Language Technologies)

ELSNET bring together the key players in language and speech technology, both in industry and in academia, and to encourage interdisciplinary co-operation through a variety of events and services. They also provide services for investors in the IT and Language Technology sector.

http://www.elsnet.org/

28.

TRANSLATION SCHOOLS WORLDWIDE

The best web site that gives you access to all Translation Schools, Universities and other programmes is: http://www.fut.es/~apym/tti/tti.htm and http://pages.nyu.edu/~rb28/t-schools.html

Below, there are some of the most famous translation and interpretation Schools and Universities worldwide.

École d'Interprètes Internationaux (EII)
http://w3.umh.ac.be/35.htm

École Supérieure d'Interprètes et de Traducteurs (ESIT)
http://www.univ-paris3.fr/esit/

École de Traduction et d'Interprétation (ETI)
http://www.unige.ch/eti

Institut supérieur de traducteurs et interprètes (ISTI)
http://www.heb.be/isti/

Monterey Institute of International Studies (MIIS)
http://www.miis.edu

29.
TRANSLATORS ASSOCIATIONS

FOR ALL TRANSLATION ASSOCIATIONS WORLDWIDE:
http://www.rahul.net/lai/trorg.html

American Translation association (ATA)
http://www.atanet.org

Australian Institute of Interpreters and Translators Inc. (AUSIT)
http://www.ausit.org

Canadian Translators and Interpreters Council (CTIC)
http://www.synapse.net/~ctic/

Fédération Internationale des Traducteurs (FIT)
http://www.fit-ift.org

Institute of Translation & Interpreting (ITI)
http://www.ITI.org.uk

International Association for Conference Interpreters (AIIC)
http://www.aiic.net

International Association of Conference Translators (AITC)

http://www.aitc.ch

L'Ordre des traducteurs et interprètes agréés du Québec (OTIAQ)

http://www.otiaq.org/

The National Association of Judiciary Interpreters and Translators (NAJIT)

http://www.najit.org

The Translators and Interpreters Guild

http://www.ttig.org

30.
RESEARCH ENGINES IN DIFFERENT COUNTRIES

EUROPE

GERMANY
http://web.de
http://www.altavista.de

GREECE
http://www.in.gr

FRANCE
http://www.nomade.fr
http://www.voila.fr

ITALY
http://www.virgilio.it
http://www.arianna.it

RUSSIA
http://www.rambler.ru
http://www.yandex.ru

SPAIN
http://www.terra.es

UNITED KINGDOM
http://www.askjeeves.co.uk
http://www.excite.co.uk
http://www.looksmart.co.uk
http://www.lycos.co.uk
http://www.scoot.co.uk
http://searchuk.com
http://uk.altavista.com
http://www.ukonline.co.uk
http://www.ukplus.co.uk
http://www.yahoo.co.uk

LATIN AMERICA

ARGENTINA
http://www.donde.com.ar
http://www.grippo.com

BRAZIL
http://www.cade.com.br

COLOMBIA
http://www.ubicar.com

MEXICO
http://www.iguana.com.mx

PERU

http://www.peruonline.com

ASIA

CHINA

http://chinese.yahoo.com
http://www.surfchina.com

JAPAN

http://jp.excite.com

http://www.goo.ne.jp

KOREA

http://kr.yahoo.com

REFERENCES

Except for my professional experience, my research was based on online research and on various linguistic magazines and newsletters. I "visited" all the web sites of the RESOURCES listed in the book together with the web sites of International Data Corporation, Forrester Research and Allied Business Intelligence, CNN and many more…

Multilingual computing and technology was the major linguistic magazine I used (numbers 35, 37, 38, 39, 40, 41, 42) as well as **Language International** and the **ATA Chronicle**.

Thei Zervaki

ABOUT THE AUTHOR

Thei Zervaki, 32, has been working in the language industry for more than eight years in five countries.

She started her career as an intern in the Translation and Terminology division of European Parliament, Luxembourg. After working in Brussels as a freelance translator specializing in European Union documents and terminology, she joined Soft-Art, a multilingual software company based in Florida, USA as an in-house language specialist. She was the Translation Category Manager for Smarterwork.com, an Internet start-up and Account Manager for ALPNET, one of the top five localization companies worldwide.

She holds a BA in French Linguistics and Literature from the Aristotelian University of Thessaloniki, Greece, Masters in

Linguistics from the Free University of Brussels, Belgium and Masters in Translation from Mons University, Belgium.

Her book is a result of her eight years of experience in the language industry. She specializes in linguistic strategy and outsourcing.